SONG OF THE BUTCHER BIRD

Love –
with warm good wishes
at the Hopkins Society

Gladys Mary

14/10/06

SONG OF THE BUTCHER BIRD

Gladys Mary Coles

Gladys Mary Coles

*Flambard*Press

First published in Great Britain in 2007 by Flambard Press
Stable Cottage, East Fourstones, Hexham NE47 5DX
www.flambardpress.co.uk

Typeset by BookType
Printed in Great Britain by Cromwell Press,
Trowbridge, Wiltshire

A CIP catalogue record for this book
is available from the British Library.
ISBN-10: 1-873226-87-X
ISBN-13: 978-1-873226-87-2

Flambard Press wishes to thank Arts Council England
for its financial support.

Flambard Press is a member of Inpress,
and of Independent Northern Publishers.

Acknowledgements

Some of the poems in this collection, or earlier versions of them, have appeared in the following journals, magazines and anthologies:

Twentieth Century Anglo-Welsh Poetry, edited by Dannie Abse (Seren); *Envoi*; *The Faber Book of English History in Verse*, edited by Kenneth Baker (Faber); *The Forward Book of Poetry 1993* and *Poems of the Decade 1992–2001* (Forward); *Journeys* by Wendy Bardsley and Laura Sanderson (HarperCollins); *Making Worlds: One Hundred Contemporary Women Poets*, edited by Myra Schneider, Dilys Wood and Gladys Mary Coles (Headland); *Roundyhouse*; *The Interpreter's House*; *Poet's England, Volume 22: Wirral* (Headland); *The Way You Say the World, a Celebration for Anne Stevenson*, edited by John Lucas and Matt Simpson (Shoestring Press); *In the Spirit of Wilfred Owen*, edited by Merryn Williams (WOA), and the *Wilfred Owen Association Newsletter*.

'From a Clwydian Hillside' won the Wilfred Owen Association Open Poetry Competition; 'The Dornier' was first-prize winner in the Aberystwyth (University of Wales) Open; 'After Edgehill, 1642', prize-winner in the Cardiff Festival International Competition; 'On Offa's Dyke', runner-up in the Cheltenham Literature Festival Poetry Competition.

The section titled 'Poems and Extracts from the Journals of Private William Manderson, Cheshire Regiment, 1916–19' is in the voice of a fictional soldier-poet.

My thanks in particular to fellow members of the Postgraduate Research Seminar at the Centre for Writing, Liverpool John Moores University, for their encouragement and valued comments.

The front-cover reproduction of a detail from Sir Edward Burne-Jones' *The Knights and the Briar Rose* is by courtesy of the Bridgeman Art Library and the Maas Gallery.

for my father

Contents

I am fire-fretted and I flirt with the wind
And my limbs are light-freighted and I am lapped in flame
And I am storm-stacked and I strain to fly
And I am groveleaf bearing and a glowing ember.

Anonymous, from the *Exeter Book of Riddles*
(Translated from the Anglo-Saxon)

From a Clwydian Hillside

Along these accessible heights the Sunday walkers
come, sharing the scenery – col, cwm and crown.
Mountains of the skyline are familiar as relatives:
we chant their given names – Tryfan, Cader Idris,
Snowdon – and those of our home hills
on which we track the path of Offa's Dyke –
Moel Famau, Moel Arthur, Moel y Parc –
another litany of labels.
A gloss on raw geology; Pre-Cambrian aeons,
shifting and settling of massive rock
in that unimaginable time before we came,
humans, with our need for names –
securities handed down through small centuries –
and our inventions which turn against us:
toxic rain, grass that kills, caesium,
genetic chaos in the flesh of sheep.

Light now inspects the folds of far hills;
shadows daub out the known shapes.
Up the cwm climb my daughters, laughing,
flushed, their long hair buoyant in the wind.
They come through the heather, calling
'We've seen a flying pheasant and two heron
heading for the Alyn.' Today they're safe
in the nursery of names – and yet
how soon their world could be denuded,
stripped to molten ash and melting stone,
new nameless mountains moulded
beneath disinterested stars.

Sekhmet at Liverpool World Museum

for Derek Ellis

Two statues of Sekhmet in the atrium
of this palace of cultures and countries,
reminders of the sun's dual power.

Goddess of flame and fire,
head adorned with a rayed disk
symbolic of consuming heat,
Sekhmet of Memphis, dispenser of destruction,
who could put out the light of stars,
wither the grass, dry the oceans,
melt eyes, dissolve flesh and bone.

Two statues of Sekhmet, side by side,
carved in durable diorite, reminders
with their amputated limbs, their fractured
bodies, of 1941, the blitz of Liverpool –
shattered images of the War Goddess,
retrieved from museum rubble.
Explosives do not discriminate.

Two restored statues of Sekhmet,
reminders that art can heal, be healed,
destroyers are, in their turn, destroyed.

Song of the Cornovii

Toadflax blazes in the rock –
a hill fort taken by grass siege

thistles rasp, bristling banners
triumph of green armour
where the last Cornovii defended:
Viricon, Vortigern gone
like the meltwaters.

Below, agencies of thrust and flow
possess the plain, more indigenous
than those tribal species, beating out
their shields of bronze, burnishing
black bowls, digging their holes
of death, lighting hill-top fires
on a not quite extinct
volcano.

More indigenous, this green army
than the Latin men, dark, supple-minded,
shivering in their new white city
under snow upon snow
trying to create internal warmth
remembering, in the mosaics of a life,
hot tiles of Roman summers

while the astral ice body
of the peak
conquers glacial ground.

Underwood sounds. Echoes of violence,
cracks, explosions, fire-bursts
fracturing clouds, frictioning water
quickening wick of war:

nothing can repair
the rift in this song,
broken tree-ribs, the shattered stone

yet nothing has been subtracted.

The Cornovii were an early British tribe living in a hillfort on the Wrekin, Shropshire. The 'new white city' built by the Romans near the Wrekin is Viroconium (Wroxeter).

Arthur

It is reasonable to suppose
such a chieftain did exist
probably in South Wales, Merthyr Tydfil maybe.

It is possible he held high military command,
and may well have rallied the tribes
against invading hordes.
Probably on a horse.

It is not beyond possibility that he fought
some or all of the battles attributed
to him, especially Mount Badon
which might have been in any of the places
attributed or claimed, especially Merthyr.

He is buried on Snowdon,
at Glastonbury, and in Cornwall
but mostly in Merthyr Tydfil.

Eidyllion

The crags of Snowdon cry
    in creaking wind –
does Arthur sleep within?
        Bones of sheep
        whiten the cwms.

The rocks of Tryfan sigh
    in shrouding snow –
does Bedivere lie here?
        Ravens rise
        at Dinas Emrys.

And the waters of Lyn Llydaw
    whisper to the shore –
does Excalibur rest below?
        Samite fish
        hide in the rushes.

On Offa's Dyke

Once a concept, now returned to concept
except where the mounded soil
hints of activity, toil,
scoopings, bendings, craft
of earthwork, unknit by wind-work.

Once a long snake, sinuous over the land,
over hill heights, above cwms:
now its disintegrated skin
is ghosted in the ground,
buried in its own earth
yet visible here and there
like the life of Offa, Mercian King.
This, in itself, evidence of him,
hegemony's power, fear –
                        the tangible remains.

Their truths the walls of history hold:
Hadrian's, Jerusalem's, Berlin's –
humanity walled in, walled out,
a wall for weeping on, a wall for execution;
and all our inner barriers, divisions
numerous as the species of wild growth
embedded in this dyke –
taken by the only natural army.

Offa, King of Mercia (757–96) built the earthwork to define the
boundary between his kingdom and Wales – both a defensive and
an offensive frontier.

Of Becket – from an Island in Weston Bay

Some, coming to Flat Holm, ask
when did these die
and why were they important?
Here, under ancient mounds
on an offshore island, lie
those doomed knights, their skeletal bones,
skulls, dust.

Others, who have consulted and trust
detailed historical texts, hold
past intricacies as present fact: cultured
they can relive the act
of murder seen as mythic drama (imbued
with symbols, it nourishes, entertains) –
sufficient to inspire an Eliot or Anouilh,
invested with significances, reverberations,
sensational as Hamlet's death,
the last sad cry of Antigone,
Gatsby's end or that of mad Macbeth.

Some wonder still,
confronted by a strange calligraphy,
why the knights were doomed,
who entombed them here
under the sea-light and the salty soil.
Those with stored knowledge tell
how Thomas fell, how Henry played
the Judas game, and these same knights
in the grey light of a cathedral came
unsheathing death into sinew, into breath,
made holy bones of Becket –
Archbishop, martyr, man.

These mounds on a mound in the sea
tell of blood lust, but of Becket's medieval dust,
nothing remains,
shrine pulled apart (there was no heart)
bones cannon-blown to Tudor winds.

While at Fontevrault lies an eroded image
of an image of a king
kissed by a lasting kiss
of peace.

Henry II was buried at Fontevrault Abbey, France, in 1189.
St Thomas Becket was murdered in Canterbury Cathedral in 1170.

After Edgehill, 1642

1. Villagers report *The Late Apparitions*

A December Saturday, star-clear,
at Kineton. Three months since the battle,
the village collects itself – Christmas
perhaps a demarcation, a control
in the blood-letting. Yet on the ridge
of Edge Hill, the night resounds,
armies grinding one against the other
re-enacting the action, re-dying the deaths.

Shepherds hear trumpets, drums –
expect a visitation of holy kings with retinues.
Instead, the spectral soldiers strike,
icy night skies crack with cries,
steel clashing and the sput of muskets.
A knot of Kineton men watch, witness;
Samuel Marshall, the Minister, says
the Devil's apparitions seize the dead.

2. A Ghost Speaks

I am unplanted, my world this waste –
the heath where bone was split, undressed of flesh,
where arteries unleashed their flood, the colour
of death. What is the colour of honour? The blue
in which we dissolve into air? The white of ashes?
Can I be woven into the braids of her hair, my lady,
or exist in the quick of my son's fingernails?
I, who carried the Standard, once drove the plough,
turning up earth, the harvest of worms. Now I envy
the seeds in the furrow, their dark cradle.

My blood is this Midlands field, this hacked hedgerow
where I lie, hearing the drumbeat of the dead,
corpses strewn rotting, graveless.
I glide up and down these rows of human manure,
the faces of soldiers like fallen cameos.
Here is Sir Edmund Verney, Thomas Transome –
they look skywards, lolling near my own wistful face.
Sir Edmund is grimacing slightly as he did in life,
Thomas Transome's skull a broken eggshell.

The brittle linnet flies from me. Dry leaves relinquish
their hold on twigs. A hare sits motionless, watching,
listening to last groans forever in the wind.
I see a troop of Horse on the skyline – Parliament's.
They charge our pikemen; now they vanish
like moving cloud-shadows across the field.
I cannot follow the clouds; I am chained to my carcass
hovering, as others are, above their unburied selves.

3. A Dragoon observes Colonel Cromwell

Like a falcon from the gauntlet, he throws off these deaths.
He tells us *Smile out to God in Praise*, for his is the sword
of the Lord. I see his horse, piebald with blood.

Heroes

from the Exhibition at the National Maritime Museum,
Greenwich, London, 2005

1. Horatio, Lord Nelson

'The bullet, the uniform and the surgeon's kit
brought together here for the first time'
in this exhibition showcase.

Not quite correct –
when the musket ball met his uniform
as he turned on the deck of the *Victory*,
Nelson knew in that moment
he was beyond the help of surgeon and kit.
They have done for me at last, Hardy.

These labelled items embody the story –
Nelson's blood-soaked vest and stockings,
his coat, emblazoned with medals,
a hole in the left shoulder
where the spine-breaking ball pierced
carrying threads of his epaulette into his flesh.

And in its own round case of gold, silver, crystal –
the ball of lead, like a full stop,
next to his grey-brown pigtail.
Let my dear Lady Hamilton have my hair.

And in a separate display, two *fede* rings,
exchanged before he embarked,
with Emma, *the wife of my heart* –
his unwanted gift to the Nation.

2. Napoleon takes English Lessons

St Helena, 1816

In comes Longwood with paper and quills,
stares hard at his pupil –
the exiled Emperor.

'Are you ready?'
Oui!

'Then we'll begin.
You will form two columns, French and English,
Write down what you have learned so far.'
Oui!

Que	that
Que	which
Que	what
Quand	when
Qui	who
Quel	what
Quel heure est il?	what o' clock is it?
Que voulez vous?	what do you want?
La femme qui est belle	the woman who is pretty
	the woman is more pretty than the man
Quand viendra elle?	when will she come?

French–English transcribed from the original manuscript

Anything to Declare?

20 November, 1819, at Liverpool docks.
William Cobbett, back from America,
deluged by well-wishers and journalists.
They followed him as he followed
his luggage to the Customs House.
Have you anything to declare?

Nothing, good sirs. Nothing.
No contraband. No opium.
The officers were thorough – after all,
this man had turned radical, now returned
from the new country, land of rebels
and misfits, a man who'd expressed
agreement with the Declaration of Independence.
Have you anything to declare?
No? Then we must search.

Concealed in the corner of his leather trunk
a last unopened package, well-wrapped
in woollen against the cold. The crowd
pressed closer. *Hold it higher –*
Cobbett urged the officer – *Behold!*
These are the mortal remains
of the immortal Thomas Paine.

Poor scarecrow Paine, lit by inner fire,
his writings touch-papers
for revolutions, for liberty and equality.
These bones had much to declare –
against slavery and imperialism,
for the Rights of Man and the Rights of Women.

As though they might scorch who held them,
the bones were thrust back to Cobbett's hands
in the slant November light at Liverpool.

Three Poems for Vladimir Zaaloff, Maître d'Armes

1. Boyhood in Georgia, 1894–1910

'He'll be a fine boy with good lungs'
Gogol

Village older than rococo,
curled in heat. Summer
stilled as a water-wheel
no water turning.
Pigs asleep in the sun
painted in light
like a craftsman's carvings
of plump angels sold
at a trestle table. Sameness

real as the unreality
of ikons, spiritually pregnant.
A scholar pushes his cart
to market, knowledge word-wrapped.
It is too hot
for clothed knowledge.

Lisp of wind, a prophetic bell
intimate winter:

first snowflakes drift
on time. We accept
a frozen eternity, learn
to dance in barns, watch
storm twisting limbs
of the bare-boned forest.
Icicles – our swords – exhilarate,
cool hot mouths, cut
the roots of childhood.

We wrestle, jump, send laughter
tolling in the rafters:
the house an empty church,
two finger-candles burning
in the rime-white window.

Nickolai lies, grinning on a catafalque:
we four, his Cossack guards, whisper
of Tzaricide, blood
on hard-packed snow, assassination
of Alexander and an errand boy,
afternoon death in a parcel –
white to red, smoke-shroud of slaughter,
men severed from horses, legs from men.

We use our legs, leap, vault
to prove they still belong to our bodies.
The Emperor has bidden you live long!
We are rebels without a rebellion.

Shadow changes on the steppes –
already shoots push
higher than the soil.

2. Duel

Weapons chosen, we salute each other,
observe politeness at the point of death
intent on graceful execution. He tests
his sword-edge; I, the tension of my blade.

On guard. The age-old engagement. One to one.
Unaware of universals, only the particulars
of tensile steel. Feint of attack and counter,
doublé and riposte, bluff and counter-bluff.
React. React. Exact.

No time to think how Pushkin died.
Children of the she-bear
(neither Russian poets nor Russian Christs) –
earth the womb or earth the tomb?

3. Captivity, 1916

Thoughts break loose
from some locked cell
streaming towards
one shining synthesis

like Tolstoy's white-breasted swallows
flying with whirling grain
out of the dusky barn at Polyana
bright-flapping in the light
above the dark and toiling peasants.

Thoughts might die
in some locked cell.

Robert Frost at Dymock, 1914

for Anne Stevenson

From America a poet came among us . . .

New England to England, a road taken,
seeking a heartland, arriving
deep in a summer shire. He'd recognised
someone on the same path, someone
like himself approaching him. Oneness
nurtured in words and silences,
choosing a way through the trees.

He held a mirror to the other's talent
brought him to the brink of poetry

and three meadows away
crafted his own, in natural rhythms
sinewy as the boughs of apple trees
in his borrowed cottage orchard
day after day under a summer haze
in Gloucestershire.

But at Sarajevo two gunshots resonated –
as from a starter pistol, nations raced to war
shattering lives, scattering friends.

When wild daffodils came again
and apples on the Dymock boughs,
he was gone – another road taken,
returned to his homeland

yet leaving a lasting legacy
in language . . .

from America a poet came among us.

Poems and Extracts from the Journals of Private William Manderson, Cheshire Regiment, 1916–19

22 April, 1916

A raw spring morning. We embarked against a wind direct
from France. I felt utterly numbed, emotions packed away
or perhaps exhausted for the time. Grey sky and matching
sea, our men silent for the most part. Some were tugging
on Woodbines all the way over; others were sea-sick; a few
of us tried to sing but this failed, our words fighting
against the wind. The threat of torpedoes tormented me –
only a month ago the Folkstone-Dieppe packet went
down. Even though we'd been assured that U-boats
wouldn't strike, who can be sure of the enemy? The
channel waters were like a skin, with shadows lurking
underneath.

24 April, 1916

A dummy hand grenade was taken apart to show us the
components. Next the demonstration, using the dummy,
and stressing how quick you have to be once the pin is
pulled. Then the real thing. Lieutenant Berry made us all
go yards back – he was going to lob it towards the distant
hedge. That moment, standing with the grenade in his
hands, he paused as a flock of birds passed over, returning
migrants; the next moment the explosion, smoke, pieces of
him scattered over the field, against the trees.

The woods have shoots tight-furled, breaking the soil
Drawn by the logic of light, not without toil
Like the worm's slow burn.
Of all earth's creatures only man's insane.

30 April, 1916

Running through my head today was that detestable recruitment song. *'We don't want to lose you but we think you ought to go.'* I was hearing it against the crackle of machine-gun fire, the thud of mortars, earth raining down. Exploding shells sing their own song, but each man will hear it differently. For me, a hissing *Shame! Shame!* Images of dark and light – erratic light bursting across the black sky, obliterating stars . . .

Today I saw a magnificent horse lying on its side, disembowelled. A dark brown Shire, its eyes open, flies settling on the lashes.

Last breath by, he's done with pain:
Grounded, life slit away.
First day of May
He should be in an English lane
Lit by Spring, gentled by sun.
I want to rouse him, speak his name.

3 May, 1916

Two nights ago we went on reconnaissance, inspecting enemy positions. A night of heavy cloud, no moonlight, only the occasional searchlight sweeping randomly across the dark, and now and then a mortar speeding like a comet across space. Unusually quiet, both our artillery and theirs in a lull. The very absence of gunfire is unnerving, the silence sinister.

27 May, 1916

A hot day and the road to Breilly was burning under our feet. I could feel the skin shredding from my heels. Mounted officers rode alongside and tried to jolly us along, but we were subdued, no one speaking except for the occasional comment. A silence wrapped us round; the ghosts of our dead marched with us those twelve miles.

Today, in the heart of a wood
I found the Green Man
Fused to the bole of a tree.
All was viridian
From head to toe, and his staff
On which he seemed to lean
Bright green.

Today, when I startled the birds,
Clearing a path through the copse,
I found a man, green
As the newly grown leaves,
Phosphorescent,
His rifle verdigreed.

11 June, 1916

Only two days left before we return to the front line. The
usual morning drill in the stableyard. Captain Barrett-
Hughes spoke to us about the Offensive and what lies
ahead . . .

This afternoon was free. Matthew wanted to go again
to the lake. It was our last chance as tomorrow will be
drill, drill, drill and pack up your kit-bags.

Lying on our stomachs on the grassy bank counting
how many water insects we could find, we noticed a
dragonfly that seemed to have been dipped in blood. On
a reed, wings glistening, about half a finger in length, its
body shone. When we tried to look more closely it flew
off, a red dart skimming over the water. 'A rare breed,'
Matthew said. To me, it seemed a portent . . .

7 July, 1916, The Somme

As here we crouch at dawn in neutral light
The sun illuminates an abattoir
Where last night's dead await us in our hour
Destroyed by mortars or by bullet's bite.

The signal sounds for our unblessed advance –
Our limbs obey; we're prey of star-crossed chance.

Worms blind as bullets searching for my skin
Twist like the wire that keeps Boche trenches barbed.
Hurled by a blast into a hole shells churned –
This crater-grave – I'm sliding deep within.

7 July, 1916

I think there is little now that I don't know about mud.
My earliest memories are of mud churned by carts, mud
mixed with slush and horse-dung. My second winter, the
ruts massive, deep like waves; I'm running, Mam calling
me back, I'm out of control, running downhill into
Everton Road, excited by the great wheels of the carts
and carriages, the freedom. A large, whiskered man
smelling of beer catches me up in his arms. Mam's relief,
her tears, her scolding. And the innocent mud of the
fields in Flintshire and Denbighshire, the ploughed fields
with their splendid, corduroy lines of earth, the regularity
of their pattern, and learning to walk behind the plough
with Uncle Iolo, creating those lines, shaping the muddy
earth. And the estuarine mud of the Mersey, with a
character all its own, dense, grey-brown, contoured like a
relief map, smelling of salt and urine and oil.

But the Somme mud, the mud of No Man's Land, is malign, taking into itself the very pith of human life, nourished on blood and bones. This stinking mud, I'm lying in it now, although this is where the earth has hardened. After the rain ceases, the clay has a chance to solidify, but only on the surface. There's a a crust forming, but underneath it the liquid clay waits to be replenished, to receive the slaughtered, to absorb them into itself . . . The mud beneath my fingernails, black earth and blood. Whose blood beneath my finger nails?

An attempt to express some of my thoughts after the gas poisoning. I couldn't think of a title, except *'From a hospital bed in Amiens'*:

Closing my eyes on death, I see the riddled bodies,
Torn limbs that once a mother bathed,
The matted hair she'd washed and combed.
Silent for evermore is the voice she loved.

Closing my eyes on death, I see my own.
Cloaked in a lethal gas, an invisible cloud,
A burning swamp in which my lungs might drown.
I'm closing on death my eyes that no longer see.

22 July, 1916, Boulogne

This hospital is high above the sea and the wind searches out every corner of the hilltop. It's nick-named 'Ozonehove'. I'm feeling stronger. Well enough to write. My first attempt since being gassed. Wheezing less, due to sitting outside most of the day. 'As much fresh air as you can get into your lungs,' says Dr Moran, our chief medical officer. But I still have nightmares almost every night, stepping on corpses, picking up pieces of human flesh. I dread the nights and the recurring dream of being

33

in a line of gassed men, all of us in our hoods and holding on to the shoulder of the man in front like performing circus animals. Always I'm unable to breathe, unable to claw the hood off because it's welded to my neck. And the stench of putrifying flesh, blood and cordite, the stink of No Man's Land, is overpowering, sickening. But I'm told by Dr Moran there are no smells in dreams. Each time I wake up I have to face the fact that my sense of smell is dead.

At last, though, my sight is improved. With the blurring and fading, I feared I'd go blind. Now, to be able to see clearly again is like a miracle. Today I looked out from the cliffs above Boulogne to the English coast. From here Napoleon surveyed his troops, encamped for the invasion of England, and he too would have gazed across and perhaps caught a glimpse of the white cliffs of Dover.

Rechristened Eyes

As if for the first time
        I watch leaves riding their own tide,
        Waves claiming the passive land.

As if for the first time
        I see clouds disperse, gather, glide
        Under the wind's invisible hand.

I look with rechristened eyes
        Can distinguish twilight from night . . .

21 November, 1916

Lines recalling my train journey from Southampton:

So here are the fields of home, the perfect grass,
Unravaged downs, orchards, meadows –
All's steeped in golden Septemberness.
I should rejoice, but hear the screams and groans
Across earth washed red from slaughter grounds
Where I saw wonder on a dead man's face,
Agony in a smile.

4 October, 1918

I was about to go up to the attic when the doorbell rang
and the post delivered a letter and package for me from
an army chaplain, the Reverend John Farrell. A shock.
Peter Sullivan has been killed. I've thought about him all
day as fierce wind tore through the trees and harried the
dark grey clouds.
   Peter named me in his will as the person to whom his
belongings should be returned: a letter I'd sent him from
Boulogne, torn at the edges, blotched with rain and dirt;
a pair of mittens I'd given him, caked in sour mud,
wrapped around his grandmother's rosary beads. Not
that these 'lucky beads', as he called them, saved him
from death.

Superstitions

Some cling to a four-leaf clover,
A special button, a dented coin –
Not holy relics, not a saint's thumbnail,
A splinter of the True Cross, or three hairs
From the head of Saint Peter.

I've seen a rabbit's foot soaked in a soldier's blood,
A black cat brooch with ruby eyes
Held by a Hun while his fingers stiffened.
I lost my smooth round pebble in the trench
When I choked in poison gas.

Some cling to a four-leaf clover.
Some clutch a crucifix.

To Private Peter Sullivan

Died 9 August, 1918, age 19

I saw your face, as pale as this frail flower:
Our lives had intersected in that hour.
You were my khaki angel, bringing hope –
Grim hope a casualty in that landscape.

Though starved of love, you had the love to give.
Now here am I, your friend, the one who'll grieve.

11 November, 1918

Up to the attic to look out on Liverpool on this first
evening of the peace. Dusk was falling and street lights
came on all over the city – houses and buildings lit,
blackout torn down, the windows liberated. It was as
though the earth and a starlit sky had been reversed.
Where before had been a vast dark pool, now all was
starred and shining. The lights seemed to me like candles
lit for those who'd been killed. And not enough candles.

I wrote a poem that night, provoked by the headlines in the *Evening Express*:

11 November, 1918

'The Ceasing of Hostilities' –
Such sibilance in the polite phrase,
As easy as a handshake
Ends a falling-out of friends.

And now there's a haunted silence,
Fear creeping away like a rodent,
Guns dumb, with empty mouths.
Now earth can reclaim the trenches:
There'll be time to groom the turf
Over the slots for shattered bodies.

What will we do with the future?
Handle it like a piece of precious porcelain
New from the clay and the fire?

Strip back the black.
Let the green of Spring be only green
Not the signal for an offensive
When innocent buds become bullets,
And flowers chalices of blood.

What will we do with the future?

17 July, 1919

The buildings are all festooned with banners and scarlet cloths – only two days now to Peace Day. Everywhere there's this froth of bunting: decorations looping lamps and balconies; shops and offices draped and frilly. At Blacklers Stores and T.J. Hughes, the windows are crammed with advertisements, Victory mugs and plates, flags in all sizes. Every house is to display at least one flag at the window. We have ours ready, bought by Father at the market last week.

Most of those marching in the Victory Parade will be those last in, 1918 men, fresh from training, cadets almost. There's widespread unemployment, but plenty of work for stonemasons and memorial makers.

The Stonemason

'My name is Legion: for we are many'
Mark V.9

He's sure of each new name he carves in marble,
Precision in his chipping out by chisel –

Each hammer tap exact to sculpt a letter.
He's not employed to grieve or show he's bitter

But merely etch the names and regiments,
The years and very finest sentiments.

He has to keep a steady hand and nerve,
Try not to picture faces young, naïve,

Clear-eyed, smooth-skinned beneath their caps and badges,
Consigned to death's red mouth, hell's hostages.

He musn't think of flesh or the distress
Of mothers, wives, or children's life-long loss.

He's now at work in every town and region
Inscribing names in stone. These names are legion.

The Black Chair of Birkenhead

An Ode to Hedd Wyn (1887–1917)

Not in green Wales, this Eisteddfod,
the National 1917 in soot-dark Birkenhead.
Far from your mountain moors, Trawsfynydd,
the clear streams, sweet river Prysor,
flock, farm and family –
yet not so far as Passchendaele.

That September the trees in the Park
were already leafed in red
when from the stage your name was called,
the heraldic call across the massive tent,
a ritual summons to claim the bardic prize.
Archdruid Dyfed, Lloyd George, Leverhulme, knew
from that audience you would not rise.

The empty Chair enveloped in black,
your absence filling the auditorium
told of Armageddon
as you lay in Flanders, six weeks dead.

Given into your family's keeping
the dark-draped throne on a cart
was processed the long lane to Yr Ysgwrn –
crested with flaring dragons
its fine oak craftsman-carved
by a Belgian refugee of Borough Road.

Hedd Wyn was the Bardic name of Ellis Humphrey Evans of
Trawsfynydd, Merionethshire, killed at the Western Front in the
Third Battle of Ypres (Passchendaele). The Royal National
Eisteddfod, 2–9 September 1917, was held in Birkenhead Park.
Hedd Wyn won the Chair with his *awdl* (ode) on the set theme
'The Hero'. The Chair was carved by Mr Van Fleteran of Malines,
Belgium, a refugee then living in Borough Road, Birkenhead.

For the Centenary of Wilfred Owen (1893–1918)

1.

'The sea is rising . . . and the world is sand.'
Wilfred Owen, 1916

In Milton Road tonight, a boy playing in the summer light
wears a crash helmet, manoeuvres his bike.
Down the slope he rides, shoots a frown at me,
aware that I'm staring at Fifty-One –
Victorian villa, the Birkonian home
of the Owens (Tom, Susan, four children).
From here Wilfred, proud of his uniform,
smartly set off to Whetstone Lane and school.
A time that was nurturing, unriven:
Sunday School at Claughton, walks to Bidston –
woods and windmill he knew well; also Meols
(his cousins' house 'Dorfold'). For young Harold
brotherly protection, inventions, games.
And boyhood joys – swimming at local baths,
riding a horse beside wild Mersey waves,
his pleasure in learning, crafting first poems.

Ten years from here, a lifetime further on,
nerves shattered by shell-fire near St Quentin,
did he, perhaps, think back to Birkenhead,
recall the mothering hours at Milton Road
where a boy, tonight, is riding his bike in the summer light.

Wilfred Owen spent seven years in Birkenhead when a boy, attending
Birkenhead Institute (1900–07).

2. War Exhibition
75th Anniversary of the Armistice, 1918

Williamson Art Gallery, Birkenhead

In this calm gallery, built between two wars,
each viewer embarks on a journey
to the Western Front.

Here in a dug-out, the chalky mud dried out,
sits Lieutenant Owen. Sandbag-shielded
wearing full battledress, he tightly grips
his pen. At the Front Line, in a lull,
he's writing letters home or drafting
verbal photographs of battle –
truths of suffering he's seen,
truths war artists were forbidden to convey.
> *They are dying again at Beaumont Hamel*
> *which already, in 1916, was cobbled with skulls.*

Paintings show British soldiers at bayonet practice,
trying gas masks, filling water bottles,
bringing in prisoners like winter cattle.
They go over the top, remain intact.
One smokes a pipe, another plays an accordion,
some are eating, a few have bandaged wounds.
> *Of whose blood lies yet crimson on my shoulder*
> *where his head was . . . I must not now write.*

Commissioned art promotes *the old Lie*
(depicting the British dead prohibited)
the corpses and mutilated are all German.
A crump shell explodes, stretcher bearers –
ants across earth's carcass – advance
> *the ground all crawling and wormy*
> *with wounded bodies.*

And here comes reveller Death, in a cloak,
striding over the duckboards, yet halting awed
before a blown-off boot.

The quotations are from the *Collected Letters of Wilfred Owen*
(1967), by kind permission of Oxford University Press. The visual
art referred to includes a mixed media *Trench Scene* by Jim Whelan
(commissioned for the Exhibition); prints by Eric Kennington,
Frank Brangwyn, Paul Nash, John Nash, Harold Sandys
Williamson and Percy Smith.

First Taste

Recalled by a World War Two soldier

In their brass bed, caged
like lions, prostrate in fever heat
Father and Mother were deep in Spanish 'flu.
I pushed my toy engine, fearing their groans
yet wanting nearness in the darkened room.
Fluff became steam in the funnels of my train,
boots and shoes lined-up were hills or towns.

Outside, discordant cheers for the Parade –
soldiers returning, the remains of platoons.
Our flag at the window was a rain-sodden rag,
red running over blue and into white.
I watched the marching khaki men,
their sudden halt at the Sergeant's shriek.
Like performing puppets they jerked,
stayed still, jumped to life again
as the gutterals pricked their brains.
So this, I thought, is 'War' – the word I'd heard
over and over, with other words,
'Missing', 'Somme', 'Dead'.

From the street, a shrill cry – *Oranges . . .*
Spanish oranges! Piled high, a cart
bright with fruits I'd never seen.
Father fumbled for a sixpence –
Sweet oranges! – it bought us three.
I felt the firm, smooth skin,
brought them to him with the knife:
he cut and offered me a half.
The centre was of blood – it overflowed,
ran down my hand.

The Dornier

A farmer's story

The moorland blazing and a bomber's moon
lit skies light as a June dawn,
the harvest stubble to a guilty flush.
I saw from the farmhouse the smoking plane
like a giant bat in a sideways dive,
fuel spewing from its underbelly.
I remember how one wing tipped our trees
tearing the screen of pines like lace,
flipping over, flimsy as my balsa models.
It shattered on the pasture, killing sheep,
ripping the fence where the shot fox hung.
Dad let me look next morning at the wreck –
it lay in two halves like a broken wasp,
nose nestled in the ground, blades
of the propellers bent . . .
I thought I saw them moving
in the wind.

If the Invader comes, the leaflet said,
*Do not give a German anything. Do not tell him
anything. Hide your food and bicycles.
Hide your maps* . . . But these Luftwaffe men
were dead. Their machine, a carcass
cordoned off. A museum dinosaur.
Don't go nearer. Do not touch.

Trophies, I took – a section of the tail
(our collie found it dangling in the hedge),
pieces of perspex like thin ice on the grass,
some swapped for shrapnel down at school
(how strangely it burned in a slow green flame).
Inscribed September 1940, Nantglyn,
the black-crossed relic now hangs on our wall.
My son lifts it down, asks questions
I can't answer.

Yesterday, turning the far meadow for new drains,
our blades hit three marrows, huge and hard,
stuffed with High Explosive – the Dornier's final gift.
Cordoned off, they're photographed, defused.
I take my son to see the empty crater,
the imprint of their shapes still in the soil –
shadows that turn up time.

'The Cow is a Mamal'

From the essay of a ten-year-old East London evacuee,
broadcast on the Nine o' Clock News, 29 October 1939

The cow is a mamal.
It has six sides –
right, left, an upper and below.
At the back it has a tail
on which hangs a brush –
with this it sends the flies away
so they don't fall into the milk.
The head is for the purpose
of growing horns
and so that the mouth
can be somewhere.
The horns are to butt with,
the mouth is to moo with.

Under the cow hangs the milk.
It is arranged for milking.
When the people milk,
the milk comes –
there is never an end to the supply.
How the cow does it
I have not yet realised –
but it makes more and more.
The cow has a fine sense of smell –
one can smell it far away.
This is the reason
for the fresh air in the country.

The man cow is called an ox.
It is not a mamal.
The cow does not eat much
but what it eats it eats twice
so that it gets enough.
When it is hungry it moos
and when it says nothing
it's because all its inside
is full up with grass.

War Story

Afternoon heat invading the factory, she felt trapped
in her turban, tied to the insatiable machine
feeding it identical parts at identical intervals.
Sun hazed the dungeon air, as in St Xavier's Church
with its soporific sermons she'd ceased to attend.
He would be writing from Ceylon, he'd promised.
Perhaps the letter was waiting at home
on thin foreign paper smelling of lemons.
Her mother would have propped it by the mirror
she always looked in, hating her turban-flattened hair,
the squashed sausage of curls. Yes, the letter
would be there. And she would read it, over
and over, like the novels of Pearl S. Buck.

The machine churned on, cogs clicking, clacking
munitions' rough music. The afternoon shift
was dull since he'd gone. The canteen . . . there
she'd seen him first . . . tall, smoking a Senior Service.
He'd smiled, suggested the pictures.
Linking he'd explained, 'I'm A1, but exempt
as an engineer. Enjoy swimming . . . sometimes cycle to Wales'.
The machine seized the rifle butts in eager jaws –
she wiped the sweat sliding down her arms.

Gone three months now. The ring he gave her, twined
and with a pearl, promised all . . . 'I'll write.
Won't be long to wait. Hitler's almost done for.'
Her screams rose above the roar
as the machine consumed her sleeve, pulling her arm
into its rotating teeth. Fastened by flesh, she fell
when the Foreman pressed the pedal of release.
'First Aid!' 'Ring for an ambulance!'
She heard their voices from a far-off reef
like wavelets around the island of Ceylon.

The pain held all her body by the arm.
'Perhaps she'd heard – it's going round –
about her Bill. Married to a woman back in Wales.
We kept it from her as he'd gone to Ceylon,
but news flies . . .'
A bomb burst in her brain. Somewhere a plane
exploded in the sun.

'No Father, No Mother, No Work'

Note by a woman who committed suicide, recorded by
Virginia Woolf in an early journal, 1903

No father, no mother, no work –
the words which Virginia Woolf
could not get out of her head
after she read of the drowned woman
dragged onto the shore of the Serpentine,
this note pinned to her dress:
No father, no mother, no work –
words which reverberate now
as I read of a woman
drowned in the brown Mersey,
disgorged on an evening tide,
nothing in her pocket, no note,
no clue to her identity:
the river released her at Wallasey.

Those words recorded by Virginia Woolf –
did they resound when, forty years later,
she herself waded into water,
placing the heavy stone in her pocket,
leaving her stick on the bank of the Ouse,
leaving her husband to mourn his release
from her madness, as the bombers,
hunting their targets, pulsed
over London, over the Serpentine,
dousing the light of moon and stars.

Sekhmet's New Weapon

6 August, 1945

Descending
through the channel
of innocent air

Descending
through the cut clouds
to the receiving earth

Descending
until it touched
the moment

Touched
the old, the young
the very young

Touched
the newly born
the not-yet born

200,000 tonnes
200,000 deaths
  and more

  this blast
  unending

N44, France: Holiday Route

Maize, wheat, vines border the road,
a straight road, one hour to Rheims,
this the country of Champagne.
The celebration wine from sad flatlands;
white of the white grape
from a blood-soaked earth.
Signposts are to cemeteries,
graves, as neat and thickly planted
as the rows of vines. No bubbles here,
no sparkle. On one side a crucifix;
on the other, a stone hand holding
a stone flame. A little stone for every man.
War is soil-deep here, though the maize
grows fine ears, the vines have luscious grapes –
all this ground seems tender,
vulnerable. Hardly breathing, not believing
in any harvest, least of all its own.

Yes, there are poppies, still in abundance;
neither are the larks absent, nor their singing.
Yet the peace now lying over this landscape
seems merely a transfer about to be peeled back
to reveal the real scene: battle, ambush.
Trees seem about to explode;
fields, copses, grassy knolls
all units in the strategy, the campaign.

While Mephistopheles drinks champagne
an angel smiles through centuries of war
over the cathedral door
at Rheims, where hotels offer the best of wine
and tourists stay, less to mourn than dine.

Ithaca–Liverpool

My father came today – an awaited visit,
our walk beachwards. Unusually quiet, he paced
the sand near the tide's persistent reach,
looking to the horizon broken by one dark ship.
'Like North Africa,' he said suddenly. 'The war.
Thought I'd never return. I used to watch
from the shore, as from a desert island,
the convoys passing endlessly
carrying soldiers to who knows what.'
His eyes held the distance: in their deep grey
was a lost boy, an Odysseus never getting home.
When the war ended, his plane, approaching
English cliffs, turned back, defeated by fog;
like a great gull banking, it landed at Paris –
a city he never asked to know. Even now,
haunted in dreams, he sees them,
the ghost ships, passing silently, one by one.

Survivor

Shuffling to his shed, Tommy Pitt
sifts the ragged peat loaves, slots
each one in the shredder, sorts out
knotty roots, some bone-white
while the rich grain shoots down
to a rising mound, tawny tobacco-heap.
Memories, impossible to shred, are knitted
into his mind's tissue, the grown-over scars
of World War Two. Today his shattered leg
aches like a limb in chill armour.

Move on. Move over. Move him here . . .
Taken from the tank, lowered to the stretcher.
Steady now . . . the swaying and jerking
across ruts to a copse. The waiting in darkness
and then a deeper dark.

His shed is isled in mist
slow to dissolve into the morning,
slipping him back to Normandy fields,
fog and foe, brambles booby-trapped.
Two haystacks move. He opens fire –
shedding straw they fire back.
His tank rips open in a metal-burst . . .

The rat-tat-tat of the shredder –
but his ears are deadened to the sound.
His deafness doesn't matter on the Moss.
Another cart arrives, the peat stacked high . . .
outside he leans against a tree,
fingers the bark like a scab.

Beginner

Taking my tranny –
no-one will see –
must have company,
the BBC!
Diggin' on the Moss
no-one will hear –
they might play the Beatles,
they're the gear!
Or the Rollin' Stones maybe –
my group therapy.
Don't wanna end up
like Uncle Tommy.

Gonna leave here
perhaps to Abergavenny
with my pal Kevin.
Kev's got ideas.

Been at the peat a year
a year too many.
Dad wants me to work
Mum wants me near.
No jobs around here –
I'll get away, get clear
perhaps try the Army
but
I don't wanna end up
like Uncle Tommy.

Once a Month

Beneath the suburban hill, near Wembley's domes
the city line sneaks, slither-speeding through.
Her cries obliterate its midday rhythms,
rise to the rafters, bisect the air –
They're writhing round my feet! Please come!
I cross the hall to her bed-sit door,
she's standing rigidly, hands to her ears –
They're tangling in my hair, around my throat!
I hold her – Lona Truding – as she shakes,
smooth her cropped head, its gloss of raven dye,
wrap her close in a dressing gown.
There's nothing there, I reassure.
Look down. You're free to move.
She follows me, sob-shuffling to my room.

Next week she's playing Beethoven's Fifth,
complains again about the dusty staircase,
asks why the bin-men haven't come,
curses as she trudges up the path –
and I know she's recovered from the visitation,
her once-monthly reunion with her past,
the lost relatives, her fiancé taken to Treblinka.

Hopton Castle, Shropshire

for Margaret Austin

Cries, now of corncrake and lark
where rough-tongued cows, low-slung,
graze in the grassy moat.
A golden retriever's on a morning walk,
his mistress strides across the meadow
lit by inconsequential sun. Silence
presses on the ancient stones, sealing
the breath of centuries, shushing
the merciless deed.

These monoliths are memorials:
the felled oak and the ruined tower,
the barred door and the broken hearth,
a weed-choked drawbridge to death.
Sunlight slants on fallen masonry,
on stones holding cries of cruelty,
the thud of cannon and the clash of swords,
mutilated men screaming in a mud-pit –
how to climb out without hands?

Religion and Royalists and Roundheads
and the rounded hills enfolding the valley
and the lane to a village which lost its men.

Between the Tigris and the Euphrates

Site of the earliest known civilisation

15 January, 1991

Today a deadline looms –
the word now laden
with literal menace.
Afternoon sun lights the ice,
frost doesn't melt,
ponds have their protective cover.
But in Baghdad the heat intensifies;
people try to pretend
this day's like any other –
traffic on boulevards,
shoppers, workers, the fatalistic shrug;
kebab stalls rotating legs, shoulders
of lamb. Keep up routines.
Perhaps the worst will not happen.

Someone in Westminster throws
red powder-paint
over the Members of Parliament.

25 March, 2003

The Menu

Breakfast – ballistic missiles.
Lunch – mega-laser bombs.
Supper – shock and awe.

The day's specials –
detailed by a dusty commentator
in impeccable English,
speaking of sides and strikes and numbers
as if it was cricket.

Anti-Environment Recipe

To make a generous helping of polluted cloud
Release your hydro-carbons into the air
Mix well with sulphur and nitrogen oxides.
Season with a little caesium.

Trap as much lead as possible in the atmosphere.
Stir the thickening ozone to make smog.
Now take your polluted cloud –
You should have sufficient to cover
300 kilometres with acid rain.

Takers

The Cockle War, Dee Estuary

The tide pulls back, exposes the beds
of cockles, vulnerable in glossy mud.
Motorbikes advance, reverberate
like low-flying planes.
We hear these daily manoeuvres
of the cockle convoy; from the cliff
we see them out there, black gulls
scavenging. They fill the gullets
of sacks, packing carts their tractors tug.

Days, months,
mining the mud
they're strung-out pegs on a line.
Marauding, guarding their ground,
they ward off incomers, compete
for the cockle coinage,
those shells of lime with age-revealing rings:
two years, one, none –
too small to take, yet taken.

Calling, one to another, they forage
in families, sons snared in their father's trade.
While nearby, on a sea-walled lake,
the leisure lads in shiny wet-suits race
clinging to their stained-glass sails.

Today, a gritty wind,
the boat-yard chinking,
all verticals an instrument.
Still the cocklers smudge the horizon –
dark question marks. Their voices
flung, buffeted like kites.

Here, on the shore,
the tide's left jokes. We find
a bloated hand (sludge-filled glove),
drowned pale hair (meshed sack-string),
swollen bladders (sliced-bread bags),
split leggings splayed across the rocks.

This detritus reminds us of ourselves –
users and spenders all our days.
We collect the spent shells. Sand,
home to other creatures, falls
through our fingers.

Tryweryn

White water fluent over rocks,
and riding the rapids
two of those fatal four, rooted in a different language.
They thrill to the creamy cascades,
the flash of light, jagged shapes of stone,
pitting their bodies, every muscle and sinew,
risking split bone, the shock of impact.

Fit fanatics, in training for death.
The river carries them headlong
innocent of its lethal burden
like the underground trains, the red bus.

Decades earlier, in a different war,
the Tryweryn flowed by an internment camp
where a young Irish prisoner secretly planned
to dip his oar in the river
of revolution. Dipped it in, and died.

These waters, from ancient sources,
slipping through centuries
beyond religions, beyond causes:
if the terrorists had listened to the river's message –
deeper than revenge,
older than Christ or Muhammad –
they might have found paradise on earth
the gift of being human and humane.

In memoriam 56 people killed in the London bombings, 7 July,
2005. Two of the suicide bombers went on the rafting course a
month before. The Irish Republican Michael Collins was interned
at Frongoch camp near Bala in 1916.

Song of the Butcher Bird

His song is broken notes, discord,
raucous, random, raw.

In action he's less bird than bullet,
striking smaller birds out of the sky,

tearing the feathers from fallen prey,
his weapon-beak rarely free of blood.

Self-preservation is all,
he stocks his larder, meals impaled on thorn,

keeps keen surveillance, iron in his eyes,
stabbing any who approach his store.

His song is broken notes, discord,
raucous, random, raw.